PERFORMER'S WORKBOOK

———

GUIDE TO TOURING

Futurehuman Corporation
96 Linwood Plz, PMB-274
Fort Lee, New Jersey 07024

Copyright © 2022 Kristi Toguchi

All rights reserved. No part of this book may be reproduced, distributed, or transmitted in any form or by any means, including photocopying, recording, or other electronic or mechanical methods, without the prior written permission of the author, except in the case of brief quotations embodied in critical reviews and certain other noncommercial uses permitted by copyright law.

ISBN: 978-1-953793-00-3 (sc)
ISBN: 978-1-953793-01-0 (e)

Library of Congress Control Number: 2022922108

Printed in the United States of America
First Printing

The intent of the author is only to offer general information to help you in your journey toward spiritual and emotional health. In the event you use any of the information in this book for yourself, the author and publisher assume no responsibility for your actions.

Aerial Fitness LLC
www.Aerial-Fitness.net

TABLE OF CONTENTS

01 - 02
INTRODUCTION
Learn how to use this performer's workbook to help your mind, body, and spirit on your next tour.

03 - 14
TIPS FOR MORNING RITUALS
Start your day right with these tips to help you create your performance morning routine.

15 - 32
CREATE A TRAVEL CHECKLIST
Don't forget anything you need at home for your performance.

33 - 49
TOURING SELF-CARE
Take care of yourself, so you will be able to perform at your full potential.

50 - 78
CONCLUSION
The final piece of advice to make the most out of your next tour.

ALOHA

Although touring as an artist was a dream come true for me and a dream that many people aspire to, I had no idea that there could be challenges in doing what I loved to do. Touring as a performer has been one of the most difficult challenges in my life. Imagine performing for thousands of people in a day, and then retreating to your hotel or residence alone. After years of touring primarily as a soloist, I have struggled and have been given amazing advice from mentors and other performers that I would like to share with all of you. I want you all to know that you are never alone. I hope these tips that have helped me feel safe traveling the world will help you on your journey.

♡ Kristi

HOW TO USE THIS WORKBOOK

This performer's workbook was created for you. Take this workbook with you on tour to help you on your journey. The key to a successful tour as a performer is preparation. Print out the worksheets and checklists provided to help you eliminate your worry as you prepare for your next tour.

HAVE A GREAT SHOW!

WWW.AERIALFITNESS.US

CHAPTER 1

TIPS FOR MORNING RITUALS

Start your day right with these tips to help you create your performance morning routine. Once you create your morning ritual, use it to feel fresh and energized in the morning.

CHAPTER 1
TIPS FOR MORNING RITUALS

Starting your day right is important for a successful performance. There are many things you can do to enhance your morning routine to get your mindset ready for showtime. You have worked hard preparing for this moment. You deserve it and should celebrate it! A morning routine can help you find joy in the experience of sharing your art and heart with others.

To begin, set your intention for the day. Your intention can be trying to do the best job that you can in your performance, making people laugh, or making people smile. Make sure your intention for the day is something positive.

Once the day begins, time flies. Set goals to ensure that you get the things you need to do are completed. If you have an early performance, you should try to wake up a few hours before call time so you have time to prepare and not stress out about being late for your gig. Use this workbook to help you create your performance morning routine. Print out the checklists and worksheets to help you stay on track.

My Fresh Morning

- Brush Your Teeth
- Drink A Glass Of Water
- Eat A Healthy Breakfast
- Wake Up Early
- Do Morning Activities

Today's Intention

Date:

Today I will be:

Today I will attract:

Today I will feel:

Today I am thankful for:

Today's Intention

Date:

Today I will be:

Today I will attract:

Today I will feel:

Today I am thankful for:

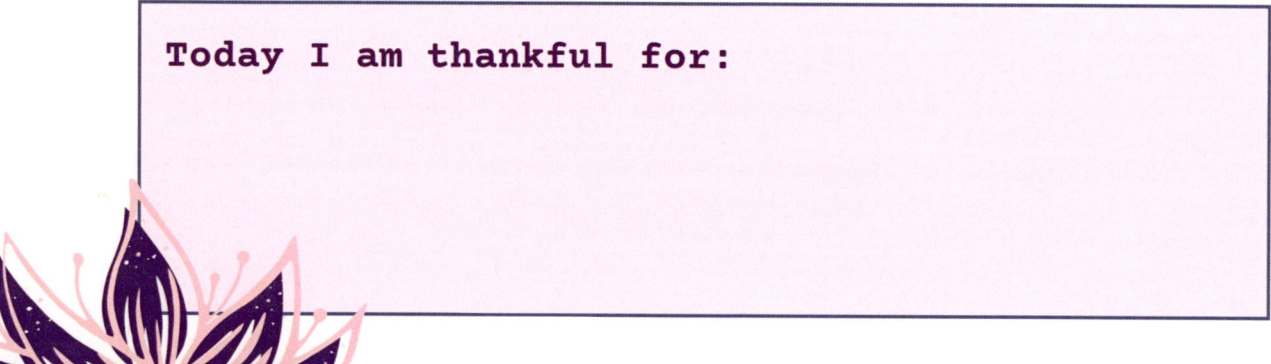

Today's Intention

Date:

Today I will be:

Today I will attract:

Today I will feel:

Today I am thankful for:

Morning Checklist

Date:

ACTIVITY	S	M	T	W	T	F	S
Wake Up Early							
Morning Meditation							
15-Minute Workout							
Morning Skincare							
Declutter Living Space							
Intention Setting							
Write in a Journal							
Night Skincare							
Bedtime Meditation							

Morning Checklist

Date:

ACTIVITY	S	M	T	W	T	F	S
Wake Up Early							
Morning Meditation							
15-Minute Workout							
Morning Skincare							
Declutter Living Space							
Intention Setting							
Write in a Journal							
Night Skincare							
Bedtime Meditation							

Morning Checklist

Date: _____

ACTIVITY	S	M	T	W	T	F	S
Wake Up Early	☐	☐	☐	☐	☐	☐	☐
Morning Meditation	☐	☐	☐	☐	☐	☐	☐
15-Minute Workout	☐	☐	☐	☐	☐	☐	☐
Morning Skincare	☐	☐	☐	☐	☐	☐	☐
Declutter Living Space	☐	☐	☐	☐	☐	☐	☐
Intention Setting	☐	☐	☐	☐	☐	☐	☐
Write in a Journal	☐	☐	☐	☐	☐	☐	☐
Night Skincare	☐	☐	☐	☐	☐	☐	☐
Bedtime Meditation	☐	☐	☐	☐	☐	☐	☐

Daily Goals

Date:

Monday	Tuesday	Wednesday

Thursday	Friday	Saturday

Daily Goals

Date:

Monday	Tuesday	Wednesday
Thursday	Friday	Saturday

Daily Goals

Date:

Monday	Tuesday	Wednesday

Thursday	Friday	Saturday

CHAPTER 2

CREATE A TRAVEL CHECKLIST

Don't forget anything you need for your performance at home. Create checklists to make sure you have everything you need. Have backups in case there is an accident.

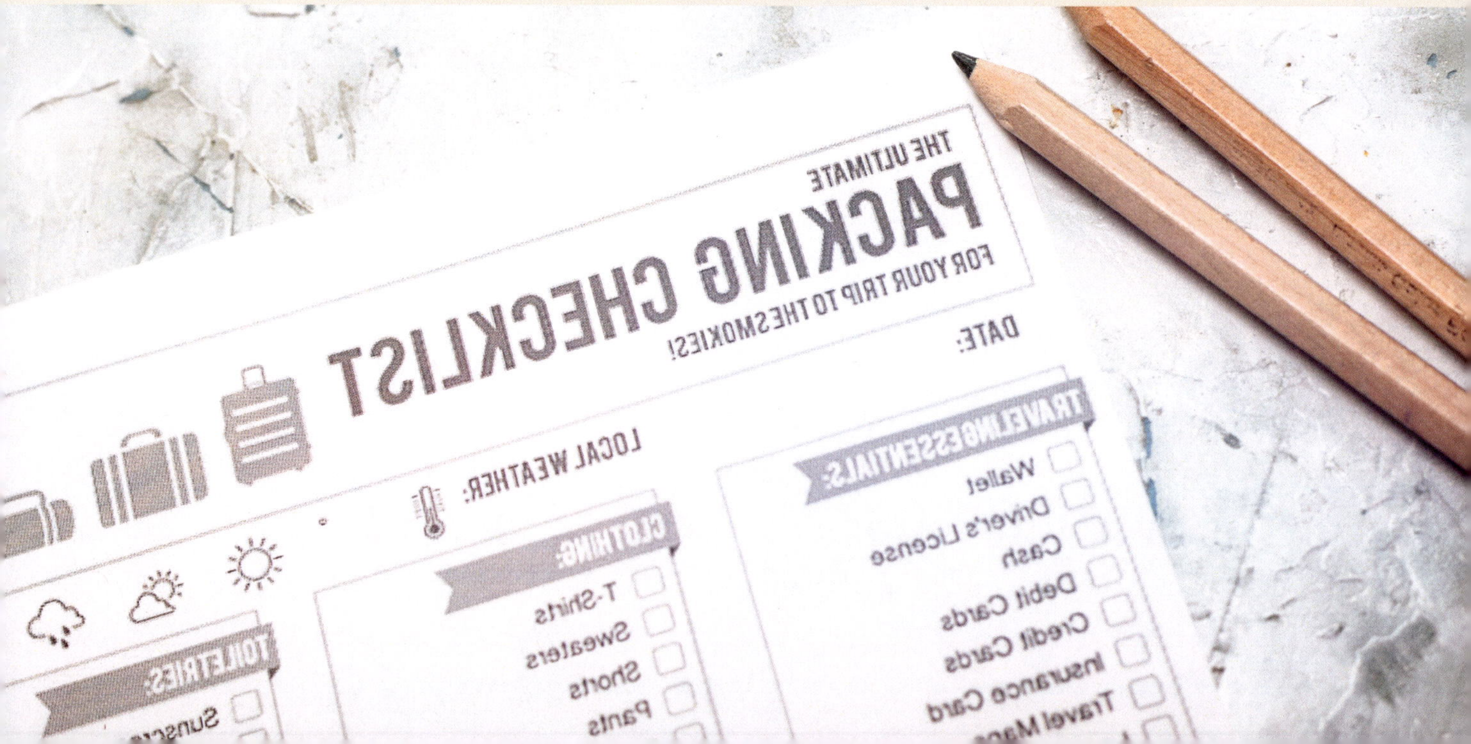

CHAPTER 2
CREATE A TRAVEL CHECKLIST

Once you create a checklist, you can save it and use it over and over again. This list may change with time. There may be something that you forgot about that you may want to add to your list for the future. Make sure to keep this list updated so you don't forget the same thing twice.

A travel checklist can consist of many different categories: clothing items, toiletries, electronics, documents, etc. This list can become quite extensive. If your list becomes too long, try creating two different lists. Create one list for personal travel items and another list for performance items. To ensure you don't miss out on any activities or sites, create your travel itinerary.

If you are traveling by plane, make sure to check out your airline's check-in and carry-on luggage policy to ensure that your luggage will not be oversized or overweight to avoid additional charges. Always have your flight information handy and double-check your departure time to make sure there are no updates or cancellations.

Travel Checklist

- ✓ Travel Insurance
- ✓ Passport
- ✓ Air Ticket
- ✓ Hotel Reservation
- ✓ Change Currency

flight essentials

- ☐ Earplugs
- ☐ Travel pillow
- ☐ Passport
- ☐ Phone charger
- ☐ Water bottle
- ☐ Universal adapter

MY TRAVEL PACKING CHECKLIST

TRAVEL DOCUMENTS:

TRAVEL GEAR:

CLOTHING ESSENTIALS:

ACCESSORIES:

MEDICINE:

GADGETS AND ELECTRONICS:

TOILETRY BASICS:

MY TRAVEL PACKING CHECKLIST

TRAVEL DOCUMENTS:

TRAVEL GEAR:

CLOTHING ESSENTIALS:

ACCESSORIES:

MEDICINE:

GADGETS AND ELECTRONICS:

TOILETRY BASICS:

MY TRAVEL PACKING CHECKLIST

TRAVEL DOCUMENTS:

TRAVEL GEAR:

CLOTHING ESSENTIALS:

ACCESSORIES:

MEDICINE:

GADGETS AND ELECTRONICS:

TOILETRY BASICS:

MY PERFORMANCE PACKING CHECKLIST

COSTUMES:

PROPS AND SUPPLIES:

MUSIC AND ELECTRONICS:

ACCESSORIES:

FIRST AID:

FOOD AND DRINKS:

HAIR AND MAKE-UP SUPPLIES:

MY PERFORMANCE PACKING CHECKLIST

COSTUMES:

PROPS AND SUPPLIES:

MUSIC AND ELECTRONICS:

ACCESSORIES:

FIRST AID:

FOOD AND DRINKS:

HAIR AND MAKE-UP SUPPLIES:

MY PERFORMANCE PACKING CHECKLIST

COSTUMES:

PROPS AND SUPPLIES:

MUSIC AND ELECTRONICS:

ACCESSORIES:

FIRST AID:

FOOD AND DRINKS:

HAIR AND MAKE-UP SUPPLIES:

TRAVEL ITINERARY

Trip Destination:

Departure Date: Return Date:

Departure Info:

Transportation:

Depart From:

Departure Time:

Gate/Terminal:

Destination:

Arrival Time:

Return Info:

Transportation:

Depart From:

Departure Time:

Gate/Terminal:

Destination:

Arrival Time:

TRAVEL ITINERARY

Trip Destination:

Departure Date: **Return Date:**

Departure Info:

Transportation:

Depart From:

Departure Time:

Gate/Terminal:

Destination:

Arrival Time:

Return Info:

Transportation:

Depart From:

Departure Time:

Gate/Terminal:

Destination:

Arrival Time:

TRAVEL ITINERARY

Trip Destination:

Departure Date: Return Date:

Departure Info:

Transportation:

Depart From:

Departure Time:

Gate/Terminal:

Destination:

Arrival Time:

Return Info:

Transportation:

Depart From:

Departure Time:

Gate/Terminal:

Destination:

Arrival Time:

TRAVEL OVERVIEW

Date:　　　　　　　　　　From:　　　　　　To:

Total Days:

Total Budget:

Country:

Capital:

Currency:

Exchange Rate:

Travel Reminder:

To-go Attractions:

TRAVEL OVERVIEW

Date: From: To:

Total Days:

Total Budget:

Country:

Capital:

Currency:

Exchange Rate:

Travel Reminder:

To-go Attractions:

TRAVEL OVERVIEW

Date: From: To:

Total Days:

Total Budget:

Country:

Capital:

Currency:

Exchange Rate:

Travel Reminder:

To-go Attractions:

DAILY ITINERARY

Date:

Location:

Weather:

Today's Budget:

To-Do List

Expenses

Snacks

$

Travel Schedule

6am
7am
8am
9am
10am
11am
12pm
1pm
2pm
3pm
4pm
5pm
6pm
7pm
8pm
9pm

DAILY ITINERARY

Date:

Location:

Weather:

Today's Budget:

To-Do List

Expenses

Snacks

$

Travel Schedule

6am
7am
8am
9am
10am
11am
12pm
1pm
2pm
3pm
4pm
5pm
6pm
7pm
8pm
9pm

DAILY ITINERARY

Date:

Location:

Weather:

Today's Budget:

To-Do List

Expenses

Snacks

$

Travel Schedule

6am
7am
8am
9am
10am
11am
12pm
1pm
2pm
3pm
4pm
5pm
6pm
7pm
8pm
9pm

CHAPTER 3

TOURING SELF-CARE

It is very important to have a self-care routine for your mental health. If you don't take care of yourself, you will not be able to perform at your full potential.

CHAPTER 3
TOURING SELF-CARE

It is extremely important to keep your mind and body healthy while on tour. Many artists who tour suffer from depression because touring is an extremely difficult lifestyle. Not only are you going to new places and experiencing new cultures, but many times you are also pressed for time. A lot of time will be spent traveling and rehearsing. Sometimes you may not like the food, there is simply no time to eat, or not many options other than fast food to eat.

Touring can cause feelings of loneliness and anxiety for many artists. There are simple tools that can help you handle the pressure of touring and performing. Creating and practicing a self-care routine can help you deal with the stress that comes along with touring as a performer.

You may also want to create a Self-Care Kit to bring with you. This could include photos of loved ones, favorite foods, favorite scented candles, your favorite music playlist, your journal, and other things that make you feel good.

5 MINUTES
Self-Care

- Take some deep breaths
- Drink a glass of water
- Do some stretches
- Spend 5-minutes organizing
- Write down 3 things you are grateful for
- Say everything will be fine

@AerialFitness

Self-Care To Do List

- **Make bed**
- **Write in journal**
- **Meditate**
- **Eat breakfast**
- **Stretch**
- **Good night's rest**

WWW.AERIALFITNESS.US

Daily Self-Care Plan

Date:

Today's Focus

Priorities

My Reminder

Goals for My Mind

Goals for My Body

Daily Self-Care Plan

Date:

Today's Focus

Priorities

My Reminder

Goals for My Mind

Goals for My Body

Daily Self-Care Plan

Date:

Today's Focus

Priorities

My Reminder

Goals for My Mind

Goals for My Body

CHAPTER 3

SELF-CARE = SELF-LOVE
SELF-LOVE JOURNAL

It can be helpful to create a Self-Love Journal to help you keep track of how you are feeling each day. Many people do not even notice that they are beginning to feel depressed. By documenting your feelings you can see if there is a pattern of angry or sad moods that go on for consecutive days. If you do notice a pattern, you can try to make a change.

A Self-Love Journal will help you remember all of the positive things that have happened in your life that day. It will create a safe space for you to create positive affirmations for yourself. It will also be a place for you to set priorities and create lists to help you with your self-care routine.

These next worksheets will help you get started on creating your own Self-Love Journal on your journey to self-care.

SELF-LOVE JOURNAL

Day: _____ Month: _____ Year: _____

Things that made Me Happy Today:

1. ....
2. ....
3. ....
4. ....
5. ....

Priorities:

- ....
- ....
- ....
- ....

My Mood Today:

Self-Care List

- .... ☐
- .... ☐
- .... ☐
- .... ☐
- .... ☐
- .... ☐
- .... ☐
- .... ☐

Dear Self:

SELF-LOVE JOURNAL

Day: _____ Month: _____ Year: _____

Things that made Me Happy Today:

1. ....
2. ....
3. ....
4. ....
5. ....

Priorities:

- ....
- ....
- ....
- ....

My Mood Today:

Self-Care List

- .... ☐
- .... ☐
- .... ☐
- .... ☐
- .... ☐
- .... ☐
- .... ☐
- .... ☐

Dear Self:

SELF-LOVE JOURNAL

Day: _____ Month: _____ Year: _____

Things that made Me Happy Today:

1. ....
2. ....
3. ....
4. ....
5. ....

Priorities:

- ....
- ....
- ....
- ....

Self-Care List

- .... ☐
- .... ☐
- .... ☐
- .... ☐
- .... ☐
- .... ☐
- .... ☐
- .... ☐

My Mood Today:

Dear Self:

Self-Love Journal

Day: .... Month: .... Year: ....

Self-Care List
....
....
....
....

Priorities:
....
....
....
....

Dear Self:
....
....
....

Things that made Me Happy Today:
....
....
....

Self-Love Journal

Day: .... Month: .... Year: ....

Self-Care List
....
....
....
....

Priorities:
....
....
....
....

Dear Self:
....
....
....

Things that made Me Happy Today:
....
....
....

Self-Love Journal

Day: .... Month: .... Year: ....

Self-Care List
....
....
....
....

Priorities:
....
....
....
....

Dear Self:
....
....
....

Things that made Me Happy Today:
....
....
....

Day: .... Month: .... Year: ....

Self-Love Journal

Priorities:

Self-Care List

Dear Self:

....
....
....

My Mood Today:

Happy ☐
Sad ☐
Angry ☐
Nervous ☐

Day: .... Month: .... Year: ....

Self-Love Journal

Priorities:

-
-
-
-

Self-Care List

-
-
-

My Mood Today:

- Happy ☐
- Sad ☐
- Angry ☐
- Nervous ☐

Dear Self:

....
....
....
....

Day: .... Month: .... Year: ....

Self-Love Journal

Priorities:

Self-Care List

Dear Self:

....
....
....

My Mood Today:

Happy ☐
Sad ☐
Angry ☐
Nervous ☐

CONCLUSION
GUIDE TO TOURING

One of the biggest mistakes I made when I first started touring was not making the time to experience the countries I was visiting. I was so hyperfocused on performing that even though I was traveling to all of these exciting new places, I did not make it a priority to actually see these places. When I would return home, people would ask me what I did, and all I could say was that I performed here or there.

Having the opportunity to travel around the world to perform is a wonderful experience. I hope this workbook helps you have the best experience with the great opportunities coming to you.

Aloha!

NEED MORE INSIGHT & SUPPORT?

PROFESSIONAL PERFORMANCE TRAINING

Many of my students have become professional performers and coaches. If you want to turn your hobby into a profession, or want to know what it takes to become a performer with the skills and techniques you have built, I will guide you through showmanship secrets and techniques to help you succeed. I will customize a special program just for you to help you accomplish your goals to
TAKE IT TO THE NEXT LEVEL!

JOIN THE MASTERCLASS

Notes

Date: _____

Notes

Date: _____

Notes

Date: _____

Notes

Date: _____

Notes

Date: _____

Notes

Notes

Notes

Notes

Notes

Notes

Notes

Notes

Notes

Notes

Notes

Notes

Notes

Notes

Notes

Notes

Notes

Notes

Date: _____

Monday

Tuesday

Wednesday

Thursday

Friday

Saturday

Sunday

Notes

Notes

Date: ....

Monday

Tuesday

Wednesday

Thursday

Friday

Saturday

Sunday

Notes

Notes

Date: ....

Monday

Tuesday

Wednesday

Thursday

Friday

Saturday

Sunday

Notes

Notes

Date: _____

Monday

Tuesday

Wednesday

Thursday

Friday

Saturday

Sunday

Notes

Questions?

INFO@AERIAL-FITNESS.NET

WWW.AERIAL-FITNESS.NET

@AERIALFITNESS

www.ingramcontent.com/pod-product-compliance
Lightning Source LLC
Chambersburg PA
CBRC091504220426
43661CB00050B/1551